POP THE HOOD

HAVE YOU GOT WHAT IT TAKES
TO BE AN AUTO TECHNICIAN?

by Lisa Thompson

Compass Point Books ✦ Minneapolis, Minnesota

First American edition published in 2008 by
Compass Point Books
3109 West 50th Street, #115
Minneapolis, MN 55410

Editor: Julie Gassman
Designer: Ashlee Schultz
Creative Director: Keith Griffin
Editorial Director: Nick Healy
Managing Editor: Catherine Neitge
Content Adviser: Bruce Jones, Ph.D.,
                       Automotive Engineering Technology,
                       Minnesota State University, Mankato

Editor's note: To best explain careers to readers, the author has
created composite characters based on extensive interviews and research.

This book was manufactured with paper containing
at least 10 percent post-consumer waste.
Printed in the United States of America.

Library of Congress Cataloging-in-Publication Data
  Pop the hood: have you got what it takes to be an auto technician? /
by Lisa Thompson.
     p. cm.
  Includes index.
  ISBN 978-0-7565-3621-3 (library binding)
  1. Automobile mechanics—Juvenile literature. 2. Automobiles—
Maintenance and repair—Vocational guidance—Juvenile literature.
I. Title. II. Series.
  TL152.T655 2008
  629.28'72023—dc22   2007035557

Image credits: Shutterstock/Brad Remy, cover (left); Shutterstock/Sudheer Sakthan,
cover (right). All other images are from one of the following royalty-free sources:
Big Stock Photo, Dreamstime, Istock, Photo Objects, Photos.com, and Shutterstock.
Every effort has been made to contact copyright holders of any material reproduced
in this book. Any omission will be rectified in subsequent printings if notice is given
to the publishers.

Visit Compass Point Books on the Internet at *www.compasspointbooks.com*
or e-mail your request to *custserv@compasspointbooks.com*

Contents

IN THE GARAGE

Engines rev, tools clink and clang, machines hum and buzz, couriers drop off packages, the smell of oil and grease hangs in the air ... it's another busy day in the garage.

As an auto technician, I spend most of my time inspecting, repairing, and checking cars. When I am not working with cars, I like to work on the go-karts that my son, Josh, and daughter, Ella, race.

It looks like it's going to be a busy week. The garage is fully booked, and Josh, Ella, and I have to prepare the go-karts for a race on Sunday.

Another car has just rolled into the garage, and I can tell by the sounds coming from the engine that something's not right. I'd better get to it if I'm to have everything done in time.

Under the hood

Cars need regular checkups, known as a service, to make sure they are running properly.

All cars need to be serviced at regular intervals, according to instructions set out by the vehicle's manufacturer. Servicing involves making routine checks, finding faults or problems, overhauling or replacing worn or faulty parts, and using special equipment and road tests to make sure the vehicle performs as it should.

When a car comes into the garage, I inspect the engine and follow a checklist to look over important mechanical parts for wear and tear.

Checklist

✓ belts

✓ hoses

✓ plugs

✓ brakes

✓ fuel systems

✓ electronics—lights, wipers, heater, dash indicators, etc.

✓ tires

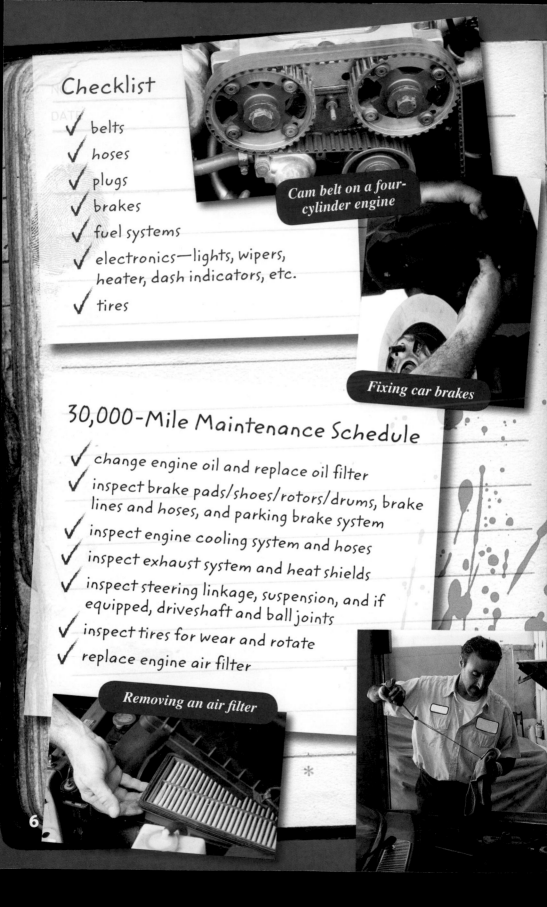

Cam belt on a four-cylinder engine

Fixing car brakes

30,000-Mile Maintenance Schedule

✓ change engine oil and replace oil filter

✓ inspect brake pads/shoes/rotors/drums, brake lines and hoses, and parking brake system

✓ inspect engine cooling system and hoses

✓ inspect exhaust system and heat shields

✓ inspect steering linkage, suspension, and if equipped, driveshaft and ball joints

✓ inspect tires for wear and rotate

✓ replace engine air filter

Removing an air filter

Inspect the Following:

- ✓ drive belts
- ✓ battery
- ✓ brake pedal, parking brake
- ✓ brake pads / discs
- ✓ power steering fluid
- ✓ brake pipes / hoses
- ✓ steering wheel / linkage
- ✓ drive shaft boots
- ✓ ball joints, dust covers
- ✓ automatic transaxle fluid
- ✓ tires, lights, horn, wipers, washers
- ✓ air conditioner

A SICK CAR

I often work on cars that aren't running properly. First I talk to the vehicle's owner about the car's symptoms. Then I take it for a test drive so I can get a feel for how it's running. Using a checklist, I eliminate the simple things that might be causing the problem.

After discovering the problem, I repair the damage to get the car back on the road again.

Talking with the customer gives a clearer indication of what might be wrong.

Suspension system

Listening and looking for symptoms

A smoking exhaust; loud, squeaky, shuddering brakes; and a spluttering engine are all signs that a car needs a technician's attention—fast!

A technician needs to know about all areas of car repair. However, in a large repair shop, a technician may specialize in just one area.

- Automatic transmission technicians work on gear trains, hydraulic pumps, and other parts of the transmission.

- Tune-up technicians adjust and replace timing belts, valves, and spark plugs.

- Front-end technicians align and balance wheels, and repair steering and suspension systems.

- Brake repairers adjust and replace brakes, brake linings, and pads.

BECOMING AN AUTO TECHNICIAN

Finding out how things work always fascinated me, and I like working with tools and my hands. Much to the horror of my parents, as a kid I loved to take my bike apart and reassemble it, just to see if I could do it successfully. More often than not, I managed to get it running as good as new.

I gained work experience at a local garage while I was still in school. When I finished school, I started an apprenticeship as an auto technician at the same garage. The apprenticeship was a combination of on-the-job training and technical classes at college.

After I successfully completed my apprenticeship, I worked for a number of small and large garages until I finally set up my own business.

My garage is very busy, and I employ four full-time technicians and one apprentice.

After school, there wasn't much time for fun and games because I'd head straight to the garage.

I'm very proud of my business.

Repairing bicycles as a kid was one of my favorite hobbies.

Doing an apprenticeship

You need to complete an apprenticeship to become a technician. An auto technician apprenticeship has two parts: on-the-job training and off-the-job training.

On-the job training provides you with the experience of doing the job and working in a real-life environment. Many larger employers have excellent entry-level positions for job seekers.

In off-the-job training, you are trained in practical skills and study work-related subjects.

Important school subjects for future auto technicians

business

math

physical science

computers

technology education

CHANGES IN THE INDUSTRY

Being an auto technician is more of a challenge than it was when auto service workers were called mechanics. Then cars and pickup trucks were easier to understand and easier to repair than today's vehicles. Many people didn't even use mechanics. They were able to work on their own cars or trucks using ordinary tools.

Modern vehicles feature special computers and other high-technology equipment. This makes them more complicated. Today's technicians often use computers and other electronic equipment to figure out what's wrong and how to fix it. Technicians also need to know how to work on vehicles that use alternative fuels and other new power sources.

One part of the auto-repair job hasn't changed. An auto technician still needs to be able to quickly figure out what is wrong with a vehicle. Computers help, but human brainpower is still needed. The technician has to know the ins and outs of many kinds of vehicles.

Just like mechanics, auto technicians need to know how to use hand tools.

PUN FUN If every car in the country were white you would live in a white carnation.

Alternative fuels

In 2003, nearly 500 billion gallons of crude oil were used to power cars, trucks, and other vehicles worldwide. Of that, 176 billion gallons was used by the United States—nearly twice as much as Europe.

In order to reduce oil usage, the U.S. government has slowly introduced alternative fuels to the public. Alternative fuels are usually a source of renewable energy or sustainable energy. Renewable energy is from natural sources such as plant or animal matter. Sustainable energy is from sources that cause no long-term damage to the environment, such as solar power.

Hybrid cars have played a big part in the development of alternative fuels. Any vehicle that combines two or more sources of power is a hybrid. Most hybrid cars today run on a combination of gasoline and electricity. Hybrid cars use less gas than other cars. They are better for the environment and better for the driver's pocket book.

Some approved alternative fuels include:

- ✓ biodiesel—produced from animal fats and vegetable oils
- ✓ ethanol—alcohol-based fuel made from starch crops like sugar beets and corn
- ✓ hydrogen
- ✓ natural gas
- ✓ propane

ALL IN A DAY'S WORK

Here are some of the things auto technicians may find themselves doing during the day:

- Organize, plan, and prioritize work

- Inspect and lubricate engines and parts

- Follow a checklist to find signs of wear and tear of belts, hoses, spark plugs, brakes, and fuel systems

- Install and repair cooling and heating systems, wipers, and stereo systems

- Test drive cars

- Solve car performance problems

- Estimate repair costs and obtain customer approval for work

- Adjust, repair, rebuild, or replace damaged or poorly working parts or units

- Use tools to test and fix car parts

- Inspect vehicles and issue road-worthiness certificates

- Document and record information

Careful filing of customer jobs makes life easier.

Other related careers

There are many other fields for a technician.

Aircraft technician: Overhaul, repair, modify, and test components that form parts of aircraft engines, pneumatic systems, hydraulic systems, and landing gear

Heavy vehicle technician: Repair and maintain trucks, buses, and other heavy vehicles

Marine technician: Solve problems, repair, and service inboard and outboard boat engines and engine components

Elevator technician: Assemble, install, maintain, and repair freight and passenger elevators, escalators, moving walkways, and other related equipment

Industrial technician: Repair, maintain, adjust, and install machinery and production facilities of mining companies and industrial plants

Motorcycle technician: Repair and service motorcycle engines and engine components, cooling systems, fuel systems, emission control systems, steering, and manual transmissions

Industrial technician working on an offshore oil rig

An aircraft technician

15

HOW A CAR WORKS

Every car is made up of hundreds of parts, large and small, that all contribute to the car's performance, safety, and handling. It is a technician's job to know all of them and how they work.

The engine

The engine converts the car's fuel into motion. Inside the engine are chambers called cylinders. Inside each cylinder is a piston that moves up and down. The piston starts at the top of the cylinder and moves down, drawing in a combination of air and fuel. The cylinder is then sealed, trapping the mixture inside.

Spark plugs, pistons, cylinders, and the crankshaft are all found inside the engine.

The piston then moves back up, compressing the mixture. When the piston reaches the top of its stroke, the spark plug emits a spark to ignite the fuel. The fuel and air mixture explodes, driving the piston down with great force. This turns the crankshaft. As the crankshaft turns, it makes the wheels go around, and the car moves.

Once the piston is at the bottom again, the exhaust valve opens. The piston returns to the top, pushing the burned exhaust gas from the explosion out the cylinder and into the exhaust pipe.

And then the process repeats itself.

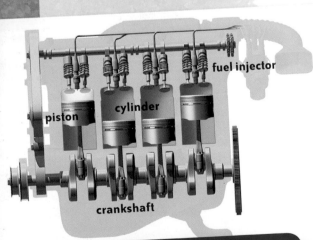

Side view of four-cylinder car engine

The crankshaft adds a circular motion to the up-and-down motion of pistons.

The gears

Gears, or toothed wheels, are used to create forward or backward motion by interlocking two or more gears together. They are fixed to rods called shafts. These shafts turn when the interlocking gears rotate. The turning shafts then cause the wheels of a car to turn around. The bigger the gear wheel, the faster the shaft turns and the greater the speed of the car. Gears help the car to travel at different speeds.

Most cars have four or five gears. Some gears are for starting off and driving slowly, while others are for driving fast or reversing.

Interlocking gears

An open gearbox shows gears in the foreground and driveshaft in the background.

Big trucks need more gears

Some big trucks have three gearboxes and as many as 30 gears.

17

The fuel system

Fuel is stored in a tank. It is drawn to the engine by a pump. The pump sends fuel to a filter, which removes any unwanted particles. It is then introduced into the engine by a fuel injector.

When fuel is ignited in the engine's cylinders, it explodes, creating waste gases. These gases travel along pipes from each engine cylinder to a front exhaust, then along another pipe to a muffler, and finally out the rear exhaust. The silencer slows down the gases rushing out of the engine, making it quieter. Fuel injectors ensure the perfect mix of fuel and air in the engine. As a result, cars use less fuel, which reduces the pollution they produce.

Fuel injectors are controlled by computers. Fuel injection was a new development in the 1980s, when computers became smaller and cheaper. Prior to that, cars used carburetors to mix the air and fuel. Most cars built since the 1980s no longer have carburetors because fuel injectors are more efficient and less expensive. However, carburetors are still found in engines designed for stock car and go-kart racing.

The brakes

Brakes slow the car down and make it stop. Each wheel has its own brake.

The brake pedal is connected to the brakes by pipes filled with a liquid called brake fluid. When the brake pedal is pressed, fluid is pumped out of a cylinder and along the pipes to the brakes. The pressure exerted by the brake fluid operates the brakes.

There are two types of brakes—disc brakes and drum brakes.

caliper

rotor

Disc brakes

Front wheels have disc brakes. Disc brakes consist of a rotor and a caliper. There are brake pads inside the caliper. When brake pressure is applied, the brake pads grab both sides of the spinning rotor to slow the wheel. This type of brake is like the brakes on a bicycle.

Drum brakes

Drum brakes are often used in the back wheels. When brake pressure is applied, a set of shoes cause friction by pressing against the inner surface of a spinning drum. This stops the wheel from turning.

Brake drum

Brake pads (left) and brake shoes (below) are designed to withstand high volumes of friction.

On tires, the patterns called tread help the car grip the road's surface, even when wet and slippery.

Wheels

The wheel of a car is made up of five parts—the nuts and bolts, tire, wheel rim, shock, and hubcap. Nuts and bolts fix the wheel to the car's axle. The wheel rim holds the tire in place. The shock allows the wheel to bounce slightly on the ground's surface, giving passengers a smoother ride. The hubcap is purely decorative. It covers all the nuts that attach the wheel to its axle.

PUN FUN

When you get your tire changed, you'll be charged a flat rate.

Rack (bottom) and pinion (top)

The steering

When the driver turns the steering wheel, the front wheels turn. This makes the car go either left or right. The steering wheel is joined to a steering column. The column is joined to a gear wheel called a pinion. When the pinion turns, it makes the rack, which is a long bar, move. This motion directs the wheels.

Lights and electronics

Electricity powers the lights, spark plugs, sound system, heater, wipers, dash instruments, and often the windows. Lights are powered from an alternator. When the engine is on, it spins the alternator around. The spinning alternator produces electricity. When the engine is turned off, electricity for the lights comes from the battery. The battery is recharged by the alternator.

Electricity lights up the instruments at night.

Interior comfort and safety

Technicians also check safety features like seats, seatbelts, driver airbags, and anti-lock braking systems. An airbag is an inflatable pillow that can be stored in the instrument panel, side doors, or the steering wheel. During a crash, the airbag inflates and absorbs the force of the driver and passengers as they are thrown around on impact. This decreases the chance of major injury.

Anti-locking braking systems (ABS) are important, because they allow the driver to keep steering when he or she has applied the brakes hard.

21

TOUR OF THE GARAGE

Tools you would find in a technician's garage

- Screwdrivers
- Pliers
- Wrenches (box end and open end sets and a combination set)
- Socket set
- Sprocket set
- Soldering gun
- Drills
- Grinders
- Crimpers
- Hacksaw
- Grips
- Jacks and hoists (to lift cars and engines)
- Lathes
- Computerized testing equipment

Screwdrivers

Wrenches—combination set

Pliers

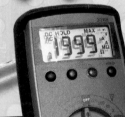

Scan tool

Soldering gun

Wrench—box end

Wrench—open end

Crimpers

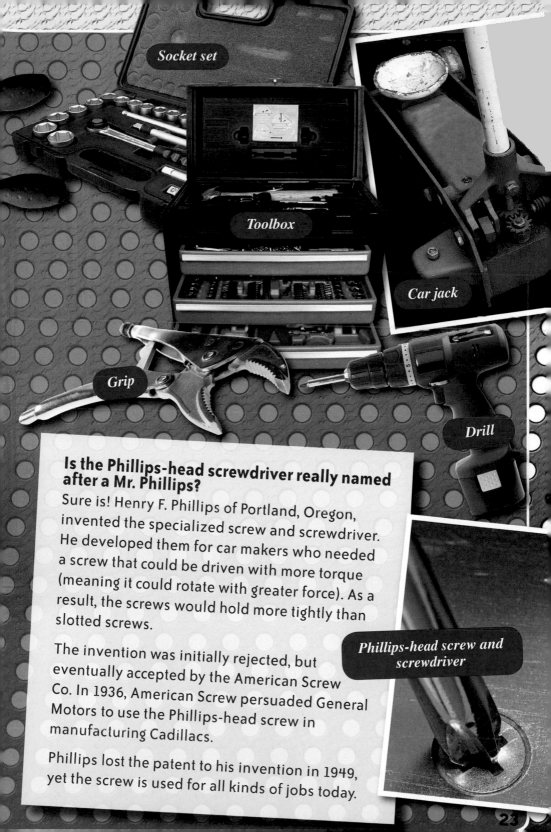

Socket set

Toolbox

Car jack

Grip

Drill

Is the Phillips-head screwdriver really named after a Mr. Phillips?

Sure is! Henry F. Phillips of Portland, Oregon, invented the specialized screw and screwdriver. He developed them for car makers who needed a screw that could be driven with more torque (meaning it could rotate with greater force). As a result, the screws would hold more tightly than slotted screws.

The invention was initially rejected, but eventually accepted by the American Screw Co. In 1936, American Screw persuaded General Motors to use the Phillips-head screw in manufacturing Cadillacs.

Phillips lost the patent to his invention in 1949, yet the screw is used for all kinds of jobs today.

Phillips-head screw and screwdriver

CAR CARE

General car maintenance is important. At our shop, we try to help our customers keep their cars in top condition. All car owners should follow these suggestions:

Not something you want to see on the dashboard during a long trip

- Check tires for the right pressure. This ensures they last longer and achieve better road grip.

- Get your car serviced regularly.

- Keep you car clean and tidy. Not only will it look good, but it will last longer.

Before hitting the road
No one wants to spend time on the side of the road. I tell my customers to check the following before heading out on a long road trip:

- Tire tread and tire pressure for good braking and handling

- Engine oil

- Water and radiator coolant levels

- Fuel levels

SERVICE REPAIR

Having your car serviced regularly ensures any problems are dealt with before they interfere with the car's smooth running.

Too hot to handle

Despite maintenance efforts, cars can sometimes overheat. Knowing what to do can help keep my customers calm. Here's what I recommend:

Pull the car over to the side of the road and turn the engine off.

Wait for the engine to cool down. This could take about half an hour, depending on how long you've been driving and how hot the engine is. Do not attempt to take the radiator cap off when the engine is hot, because scalding coolant could spray out and burn you.

Be kind to the environment by washing your car on grass. This keeps polluted water from running into storm drains and getting into local water supplies.

When the engine is cool, pop the hood and check the coolant level in the radiator. If coolant is needed, refill the radiator and drive to the nearest garage to check that everything is OK.

If the problem is not caused by a low coolant level, call a towing service or the police, who can arrange for help.

Checking air pressure

When the car won't start

Even if the car won't start, a few things can be checked before calling a technician.

- Check the fuel gauge on the dashboard to see if you have gas. (You'd be surprised how many people drive around on almost empty!)

- Check to ensure the battery terminals are clean and tight.

- Check the battery for power. If the lights, dashboard indicators, or stereo is working, you have power. If the lights are dim, you may not have enough power to start the car. If this is the case, you'll need to recharge the battery.

- If you have a flat battery, find someone with another car and some jumper cables. Connect the jumper cables to both batteries, connecting positive to positive and negative to negative. Start the car with power, and then start the car with the flat battery. Let both cars run for around five minutes before you disconnect the jumper cables. Take the flat battery for a drive to charge it up.

- If the car still won't start, call for expert help.

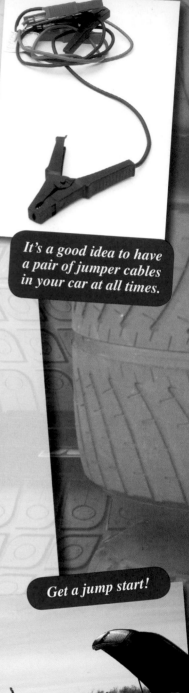

It's a good idea to have a pair of jumper cables in your car at all times.

Get a jump start!

Remove the hubcap.

How to change a tire

Make sure you are off the road. Park on a safe, level surface. Ensure the car handbrake is on, and block the other wheels. Get the spare tire, car jack, and lug wrench out of the car.

Remove the hubcap, then loosen the lug nuts in diagonal pairs using the lug wrench. (Working in diagonal pairs keeps the wheel more stable while you are working.) Raise the car with the car jack. Take the old tire off and put on the new tire. Put the lug nuts on and tighten them in diagonal pairs using the lug wrench. Let the jack down until the wheel is just touching the ground.

Tighten the lug nuts again to make sure they are secure. Finish lowering the vehicle and remove the jack. Put the tools and damaged tire in the trunk.

Get your tire repaired. You don't want to get caught without a spare.

Raise the car with the car jack.

Remove the lug nuts.

Remove the old tire.

After putting on the new wheel, tighten the lug nuts using the lug wrench.

27

CARS WITH SPEED

Cars are not just used for transportation, they are also used for sport and fun.

Racing cars

Racing cars are built for maximum speed and the best possible road handling. Types of racing include Formula One, stock car, rally, and drag.

Formula One

Formula One, also known as Grand Prix racing, is the fastest and most powerful kind of track racing. It is the highest class of car racing in the world. Cars can travel up to nearly 200 miles per hour on straight sections of the track.

Stock car racing

Stock car racing is very popular. Stock cars are purpose-built racing cars that have the basic steel frame of a passenger car. Car speeds can reach up to 200 mph.

Grand Prix racing began in France in 1894.

The frame of a stock car resembles a passenger car frame.

Rally car racing

Rally car driving is tough on cars. It's different from other forms of car racing because it takes place not on a circuit but on sand, mud, and snow, all with many obstacles.

All cars follow the same route but start at different times. The course is divided into separate sections known as special stages. There is a time limit for each stage. The winner of the rally has the fastest overall time.

PUN FUN The failure of the vehicle's brakes caused an instant ram-ification.

Drag racing

Drag racing involves starting from a dead stop and racing on a straight and level course of either a quarter-mile (1,320 feet) or an eighth-mile (660 feet). Drag racing started in the United States and is now popular around the world.

WORKING ON RACE CARS

Some auto technicians end up working in the exciting world of auto racing. Every race car team has a group of dedicated technicians who work long hours repairing, rebuilding, maintaining, and servicing race cars between races.

Formula One racing is tough on the car.

Crowded pit stop

At a Formula One pit stop, there can be as many as 18 technicians, each with a specific job to do. There are three people per wheel—one to remove the locking nut, one to remove the old tire, and a third to roll in the new tire. Two people handle the fueling rig. One person at each end operates the manual jack. One stands by the starter in case the engine stalls. And another holds a sign paddle in front of the driver telling him when it is safe to go back on the course.

The driver usually waits in the car while the pit crew technicians work.

Imagine being a technician in a racing car pit crew

The driver can feel that his tires are wearing down. He radios ahead to the pit crew so you and the rest of the technicians are ready when he pulls up. As a team, you race out to jack up the car, loosen the lug nuts, change the tires, and tighten the nuts again. You do it all in less than eight seconds!

It is also your job to use sign boards to let the driver know his position and how many laps are left in the race.

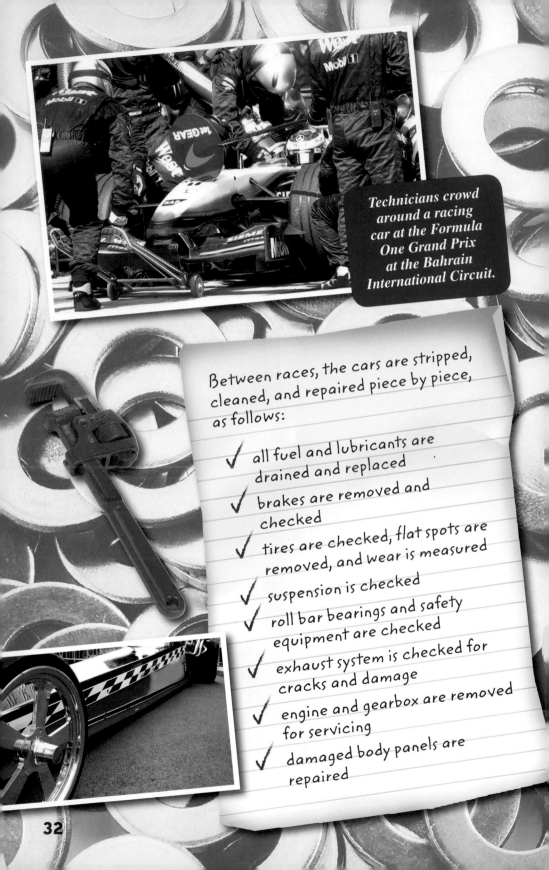

Technicians crowd around a racing car at the Formula One Grand Prix at the Bahrain International Circuit.

Between races, the cars are stripped, cleaned, and repaired piece by piece, as follows:

✓ all fuel and lubricants are drained and replaced

✓ brakes are removed and checked

✓ tires are checked, flat spots are removed, and wear is measured

✓ suspension is checked

✓ roll bar bearings and safety equipment are checked

✓ exhaust system is checked for cracks and damage

✓ engine and gearbox are removed for servicing

✓ damaged body panels are repaired

Bringing technology to the track

An important tool for race technicians and drivers is a data acquisition system. It lets both the driver and the technicians know how the car is performing. It records and reports data while the car is being driven. The data is downloaded from the car to a laptop in the pit and analyzed after each session.

The data is downloaded to a laptop for further processing by the pit crew.

With this technology, crew members can review data from hundreds of sensors mounted on the car. The system measures wheel speed, throttle position, steering angle, brake pressure, and suspension. It also records engine oil pressure, oil temperature, water temperature, gearbox temperature, and the fuel-to-air ratio.

All this information helps the technicians and the drivers set the car up for what they hope will be the perfect winning lap.

When conditions are wet and dangerous, the system lets the crew know how the car is performing, allowing the driver to better handle the car.

33

GO-KART RACING

Many of the best professional racing car drivers started their careers through go-kart racing as teenagers. It is the perfect starting place for anybody interested in motor racing. The speeds are not as fast as other types of motor racing, and it's generally not as dangerous.

Race speeds can be anywhere from 20 to 100 mph. Karts were created in the United States in the 1950s post-war period by airmen as a way to pass spare time. Kart racing has since spread to other countries and is now popular in Europe.

Go-karts are exciting to drive. In karting, competitors race around a small track. There are professional races, but there are also lots of tracks where people can drive go-karts for fun.

In a go-kart, you have a greater sensation of speed than in an ordinary vehicle because you are much closer to the ground. How fast you go depends on the type of kart, the length of the track, and the class you are racing in.

In racing, go-karts are classified according to the size of the engine. Officials, called scrutineers, inspect and weigh the go-karts before and after the race to make sure they are in good condition and meet the requirements for racing.

Placing old tires along the track cushions any impact in case a driver veers off the track.

To keep the karts safe and performing at their best, I check each motor thoroughly. I also check the karts for the following:

✓ cracks
✓ loose bolts and fasteners
✓ frayed, weak, or faulty cables
✓ worn brake pads
✓ worn tires
✓ faulty pedals
✓ worn wheel bearings
✓ cracked steering rods
✓ kinked cables
✓ loose exhaust
✓ leaking fuel and tank line
✓ bent tire rims
✓ worn chains and sprockets

Cracks in the body of the kart need to be repaired to prevent further damage.

The main components of a go-kart are a fiberglass body, seat, steering wheel, frame, engine, and wheels.

fibreglass body

steering wheel

seat

wheels

frame

wheels

engine

35

GETTING THE GO-KART READY FOR RACE DAY

Monday

Josh and Ella arrive at the workshop after school to clean their karts after a weekend of hectic racing. They want to make sure their karts are in the best possible condition. This improves their chances of winning. They realize they're very lucky to have an auto technician for a dad!

I carefully go over the karts and assess what needs to be fixed or replaced. Josh and Ella tell me about any problems they noticed in their last race.

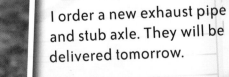

Josh and Ella can be quite competitive, but usually in a good-natured way.

Josh's kart has a bent front stub axle from a crash he had, and Ella's kart has a fractured exhaust pipe that will need to be replaced. I'm also going to install a new carburetor in Ella's kart because the old one is worn out and is not working as effectively as it should.

I order a new exhaust pipe and stub axle. They will be delivered tomorrow.

The stub axle on Josh's kart needs replacing.

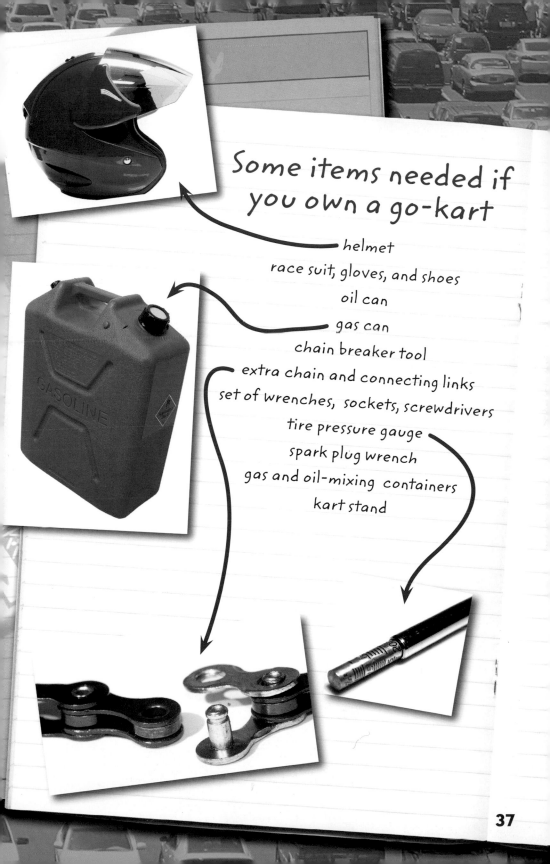

Some items needed if you own a go-kart

- helmet
- race suit, gloves, and shoes
- oil can
- gas can
- chain breaker tool
- extra chain and connecting links
- set of wrenches, sockets, screwdrivers
- tire pressure gauge
- spark plug wrench
- gas and oil-mixing containers
- kart stand

Tuesday

On Tuesday afternoon, I repair the karts with Josh and Ella's help. I install Josh's new axle stub, which has been delivered along with Ella's exhaust pipe. His kart also needed a wheel alignment and some body work repair.

Ella and I fitted the new carburetor to her kart. I also replaced a worn out fuel line.

Wednesday

After school, Josh, Ella, and I take the karts to the local track to see how they perform following the repairs. I make adjustments to Ella's carburetor and the steering on Josh's kart.

Saturday

We go to the race track for a practice session. We make notes about the track on a track map. Josh and Ella make a note of where their karts handled well and where they didn't by putting smiley and grumpy faces on the map. We discuss what their karts felt like to drive. I see what changes I can make to help them improve the kart's handling. Some of the corners on the track have names that give you an idea of the kind of experience they are in for.

Josh and Ella head to the shop right after school.

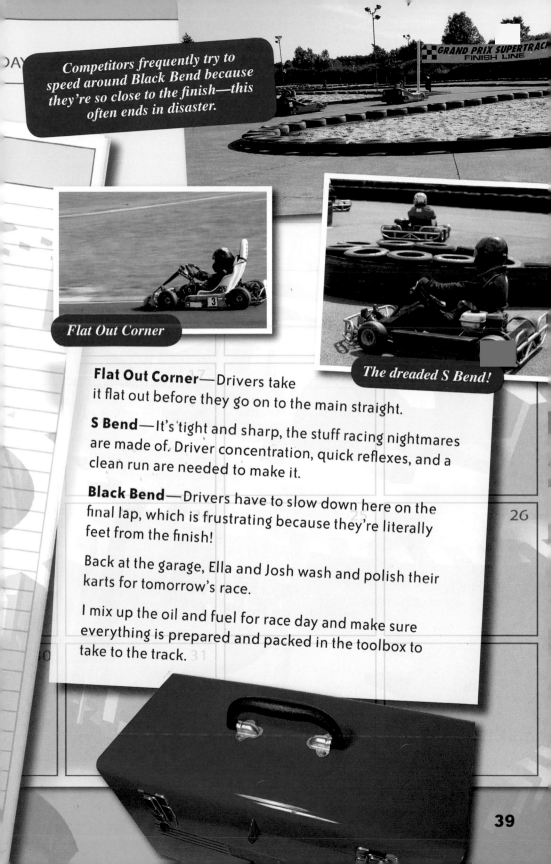

Competitors frequently try to speed around Black Bend because they're so close to the finish—this often ends in disaster.

GRAND PRIX SUPERTRACK
FINISH LINE

Flat Out Corner

The dreaded S Bend!

Flat Out Corner—Drivers take it flat out before they go on to the main straight.

S Bend—It's tight and sharp, the stuff racing nightmares are made of. Driver concentration, quick reflexes, and a clean run are needed to make it.

Black Bend—Drivers have to slow down here on the final lap, which is frustrating because they're literally feet from the finish!

Back at the garage, Ella and Josh wash and polish their karts for tomorrow's race.

I mix up the oil and fuel for race day and make sure everything is prepared and packed in the toolbox to take to the track.

IT'S RACE DAY

The field quickly spreads out after crossing the starting line.

A waved yellow flag means extreme caution should be taken ahead.

Sunday: Race Day

7:00 A.M.   Arrive at the track. Set up the pit tent and put the karts on their stands so they are at a good working height for any last-minute tweaking.

7:15 A.M.   Josh and Ella register for their races.

8:00 A.M.   Kart is checked by the scrutineer and weighed in.

9:30 A.M.   First race

10:30 A.M.   Second race

11:30 A.M.   Third race

4:00 P.M.   Final

Race one

All the karts set a speeding pace off the grid. Five go-karts never make it through S Bend on the fourth lap. They are now out of the race. Josh and Ella weave their way through the mayhem and manage to stay in the race. Another driver loses his kart on Flat Out Corner in the seventh lap. Josh and Ella drive a steady race and come in sixth and eighth places.

Back in the pits

I go over the karts for wear and tear and refuel them.

Race two

The first corner takes out several of the race favorites. Go-karts spin and slide everywhere. Josh and Ella were slow off the start and somehow manage to slip through with Josh taking the lead! With three laps to go, Ella overtakes him on S Bend after Josh slides wide. Ella roars home to take first place, with Josh not far behind in second.

Back in the pits

I go over the go-karts, paying special attention to checking the brakes. (Josh said brake problems may have been the reason he slid wide on S Bend.) I refuel both go-karts.

Race three

All the drivers know this is an important race if they want to make it to the final. You can feel the tension before the race. Josh and Ella are both slow off the grid. By the second lap, they are only in 10th and 11th places. Josh finds some speed halfway through the race and crisscrosses through the field with Ella on his tail. He manages to survive a bump that almost throws him out of the race just before Black Bend. The race leader, Dale Gibbons, makes a huge mistake on the second to the last lap and spins off the track. Ella and Josh finish in third and fourth places. They are both in the final!

Back in the pits

I check both karts and refuel them. We talk driving tips and race tactics for the final.

Ella is determined to beat her big brother in the next race!

Final lap

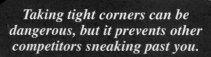

Taking tight corners can be dangerous, but it prevents other competitors sneaking past you.

The final

Right from the start, the battles are on. One of the race favorites, Greg Bailey, drops a chain on the second lap and is out of the race. Josh skids out of a corner in the sixth lap but somehow manages to stay in the

Competition is fierce in the semis and finals.

race. Ella does well to make her way to fourth place by the fifth lap. Josh drives hard and makes his way through the pack. With three laps to go, Ella and Josh are fighting it out for third and fourth places. Black Bend takes out the kart in second place with one lap to go. Ella and Josh sprint home with Ella barely missing first place. Josh came in third.

It's been an exciting day at the track. I'm happy with the way Josh and Ella drove and very happy that the go-karts managed to come away from the meet without any major damage. But there is still work to do to get them ready for the next race. It's scheduled for mid-week, so it looks like it's going to be a busy couple of days in the garage.

Better get cracking … pass me a combination wrench and a Phillips-head screwdriver, would you, please?

Ella missed first place by a split second.

JOB OPPORTUNITIES

Follow these steps to become an auto technician

Step 1 Start preparing for an automotive career in school by concentrating on business, metalwork, math, science, and computer science, because these are very useful subjects for auto technicians.

Step 2 Look for apprenticeship and training programs. Some larger employers offer programs for entry-level workers. An apprenticeship combines practical, paid work with structured training to give you both experience and certification.

Step 3 Many technicians start off by getting work experience in a garage and then studying for certification from a vocational or technical school.

Step 4 Look for an employer who offers opportunities for continued professional development through training.

Step 5 Tell prospective employers about specialized interests and skills you have, such as experience in using advanced computerized diagnostic systems.

Step 6 Being a successful technician comes from good working relationships with your employer and establishing a good reputation in the industry. And remember that you'll need to invest in a personal tool kit, so it's best to begin this as early as possible.

PUN FUN A technician bolted out of his shop to find some nuts only to wrench his back.

Opportunities for auto technicians

With the changes in automotive technology, there are now more electronic controls and computers fitted to vehicles. As a result, there are opportunities to become specialized in these areas.

- You could work for a small local garage or for a much larger organization that owns and manages a chain of garages.

- You could decide to open and run your own business.

- Auto technicians may progress to positions such as service managers.

Character traits and skills

If you ...

- Enjoy practical and manual work
- Are handy with tools
- Have a technical aptitude
- Can problem solve
- Are physically fit
- Have normal eyesight and hearing

... then being an auto technician could be the career for you.

FIND OUT MORE

IN THE KNOW?

- Employment opportunites are expected to increase as fast as the average overall job growth through the year 2014.

- The U.S. Department of Labor advises that formal training is the best preparation for a career as an auto technician.

- Many auto technicians earn certification from the National Institute for Automotive Service Excellence. Certification requires at least two years of service and a passing score on an exam.

- In recent years, more than 16 percent of auto technicians were self-employed.

- Average hourly wage in 2006 was $17.34. The lowest 10 percent earned less than $9.17, and the highest 10 percent earned more than $27.22 per hour.

FURTHER READING

Bickerstaff, Linda. *Cool Careers Without College for People Who Love to Fix Things*. New York: Rosen Publishing Group, 2004.

Newton, Tom. *How Cars Work*. Vallejo, Calif.: Black Apple Press, 1999.

Stewart, Mark. *Auto Racing: A History of Fast Cars and Fearless Drivers*. New York : Franklin Watts, 1998.

Weintraub, Aileen. *Auto Mechanic*. New York: Children's Press, 2004.

Zuehlke, Jeffery. *Muscle Cars*. Minneapolis: Lerner Publications, 2007.

ON THE WEB

For more information on this topic, use FactHound.

1. Go to *www.facthound.com*
2. Type in this book ID: 0756536219
3. Click on the *Fetch It* button.

GLOSSARY

apprenticeship—learning a skill by receiving on-the-job training from a skilled professional

aptitude—natural ability; the ability to learn quickly

brake fluid—fluid used in a car's brake system to transmit pressure to the braking mechanism near the wheels

brake pads—pads that apply friction to both sides of the brake disc

caliper—device on disc brakes that holds the brake pads

coolant—mixture of water and antifreeze circulated through the engine to carry off heat produced by the engine

dashboard—panel located under the windscreen, containing indicators and dials such as the fuel gauge and speedometer

entry-level job—low-level job in which an employee gains experience and skills

exhaust pipe—pipe used to guide waste exhaust gases away from a controlled combustion inside an engine

fuel injector—electronically controlled small valve that controls the amount of fuel entering an engine

fuel system—system that delivers fuel to the engine, consisting of a fuel tank, fuel filter, fuel pump, and fuel injector

jumper cables—cables used to start a car without power by conducting electrical current from one car battery to another

pinion—toothed wheel, usually made of steel, with a small number of teeth

rack—bar with teeth on one side to mesh with the teeth of a pinion

radiator—part of the vehicle through which the coolant flows so that it can be cooled

rotor—disc-shaped part of a brake assembly

service—to provide the required maintenance or repair

suspension system—system of springs and shock absorbers used to suspend a vehicle's frame, body, and engine above the wheels

technical—having to do with machines or computers

technician—person who is trained or skilled in a technical area

INDEX

Look for More Books in This Series: